Dr. Christine Jaitner

Alpine Flowers

SIGHTING AND ENJOYING

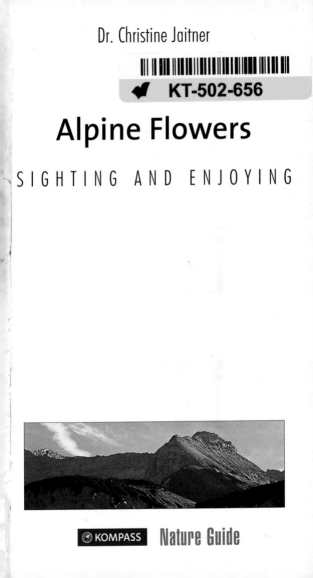

KOMPASS **Nature Guide**

The author **Dr. Christine Jaitner**, born 1952, studied zoology and systematic botany at Innsbruck University. She received her Ph. D. in the field of protozoology.

Impressum
72 color photos
2 color plates
2 illustrations

Text: Dr. Christine Jaitner, Patsch
English translation: Mary Heany Margreiter, Innsbruck
Color plates and Illustrations: Heinz Schwanninger, Absam
Management and Editing: Reinhard Strohmeier,
                                        KOMPASS-Karten GmbH

Color Photos:
Front Cover/Back Cover: Alpenroses (Bildagentur Dr. Wagner)
Baier: 65 • Bernardinatti: 66 • Bildagentur Fiebrandt: 8 ,11, 13, 14, 15, 16, 17, 20, 21, 23, 24, 26, 28, 31, 32, 33, 34, 38, 44, 47, 52, 53, 58, 59, 63, 68, 74, 76, 77 • Brüßler: 9, 12, 36, 54, 67, 73 • Geiersperger/Bildagentur Dr. Wagner: 10, 29, 40, 46, 60, 64, 69 • Geissler: 25, 28, 49 , 61 • Haas: 19, 22, 57 • Hage: 35, 42 • Limbrunner: 18, 27, 30, 37, 39, 41, 43, 45, 50, 51, 53, 56, 62, 70, 71, 75 • Verkehrsverein Sonnenalpe/Nassfeld: 72 • Zeininger: 55.

© **KOMPASS - Karten GmbH**
    A-6063 Rum/Innsbruck, Austria
    Fax 0043 (0)512/26 55 61-8
    e-mail: kompass@kompass.at
    www.kompass.at

5th edition 2009

Phototype: Raggl Supertype GmbH&Co. KG, Innsbruck
Reproductions: Tiroler Repro Druckformen GmbH, Innsbruck
Printed by: Printers s.r.l., Trento

Publisher´s No.1300
ISBN 978-3-85491-592-8

Dear Nature Friend,

Everyone who likes being outdoors and appreciates flora and fauna will enjoy identifying the different plants and animals. This book was conceived to not overburden the nature-watcher in his identification and is intentionally concise and easy to read.

In this KOMPASS Nature Guide you will find 70 of the most common and abundant Alpine plants. It should be mentioned that these plants also occur in other mountainous regions of Europe. Since a solely textual description of the individual plants is not sufficient to guarantee proper identification, the color photos were so chosen to show the plants in their true colors and natural surroundings. The plants are primarily ordered according to the color of their flowers. Within this color group, they are systematically classified.

The names are given both in English (for example Least Primrose) and according to the „binary nomenclature" defined by Linné, namely the genus (primula) and species (minima). Several genera (or genuses) from a family (-aceae) and several families an order (-ales). The orders make up the classes (-atae). These are grouped in sections and the kingdom.

Since each plant is known under a variety of names in English, this guide uses the most common name. This is followed by the plant's scientific name, the family to which it belongs, characters, habitat, distribution and special remarks.

The listings "Date Seen" and "Place" will give you the chance to note your observations an the spot.

Enjoy the flora of the Alps!

Dr. Christine Jahre

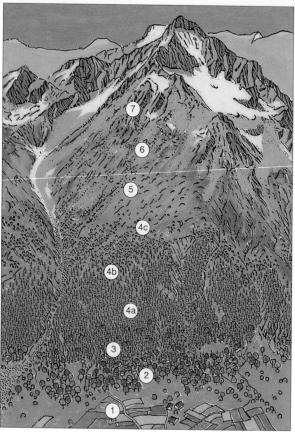

1 **Planar Belt:** grain fields
2 **Colline Belt:** deciduous forests, meadows
3 **Mountain Belt:** mixed forests
4a **Lower Subalpine Belt:** coniferous forests to tree line
4b **Mid- Subalpine Belt:** knee-timber belt
4c **Upper Subalpine Belt:** dwarf-shrub belt with berries
5 **Alpine Belt:** Alpine grasslands
6 **Subnival Belt:** pioneer grasslands belt
7 **Nival Belt:** cushion grasslands belt with mosses and lichen

4

Altitude Belts of the Alps

Altitude and dropping temperatures determine the following **altitude belts** or vegetation belts:

Planar Belt: grain field, residual forests

Colline Belt: oak and hornbeam woods, meadows, vines

Mountian Belt: 800 – 1000 m, red beeches, spruce, larches

Subalpine Belt: 1600 – 2000 m
a) Lower Subalpine Belt:
   last coniferous forests (spruce, larches, arolla pines)
   before tree line
b) Mid-Subalpine Belt:
   knee pines
c) Upper Subalpine Belt:
   dwarf-shrub belt with crowberry, magnolia vine, cranberry

Alpine Belt: approx. 1300 m, belt of Alpine grasslands, pastures

Subnival Belt: approx. 2600 – 2800 m, pioneer grasslands belt

Nival Belt: cushion plant belt and cryptogamic belt (mosses, lichen, algae)

Vegetation Forms in the Various Habitats

Rock crevices:	temperature-insensitive, resistant to snow and sand storms, insensitive to dryness, cushion plants rosettes, dwarf subshrubs
Screes:	debris creeper, debris wanderer with taproot, debirs coverer with rooting branches, debirs holder with firm grasp
Snowbeds:	extremly short vegetation peroid, green parts and flowers often spend winter under the snow, dwarf growth, dwarf willows, least willows
Springs:	moss, saxifrages, butterworts, marsh marigold, birdseye primrose, cotton sedge

High-Alpine Grasslands:	many plants with evaporation protection such as hairy leaves, mountian avens, saxifrages, moss campion, edelweiss, trumpet gentain
Mats:	cultivated meadows, corcus, grasses, dandelion
Tall Herb Communities:	common monkshood, thistle, helleborine
Overfertilized Alms:	over-fertilized soils on alpine pasture, docks
White Bent Grasslands:	result of overgrazing, white bent
Dwarf Shrub Heath:	woody plants, cranberry, bearberry, alpenrose
Knee-Timber Thicket:	garland flower, alpine clematis, mountian pine, green alder

Plants Parts

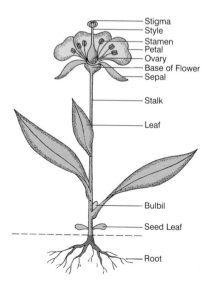

6

Definitions

Completely protected: These plants must not be picked, damaged or destroyed. In their fresh state they may not be transplanted, purchased, transported or sold. This protection covers all parts of the plant.

Protected: These plants are completely or partially protected, depending on the country where they are found.

Partially proteceted: The protection is limited to certain peroids, develompment forms, locations and parts and excludes commercial trade or collecting.

Endemic: plant only occurs within a certain region.

Rhizome: underground, horizontal root.

Monocious: male and female flowers on the same plant.

Dioecious: male and female plant.

Bisexual: one flower has male and female plant parts.

♂ : male

♀ : female

Cluster of Rush Flowers: Flowers of the rushes and sedges; lower branches of the flowers protrude above the upper ones.

† poisonous
⚠ protected

Flower Colors:

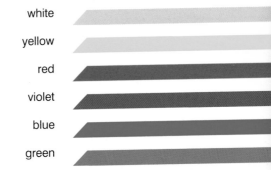

white

yellow

red

violet

blue

green

7

Alpine Buttercup

Ranunculus alpestris   Buttercup Family; †

Characters: perennial, five white petals, solitary flower, petals
and sepals fall off soon, leaves 3 – 5 -lobed; lobes palmately
lobed, stems hairless, height 5 – 15 cm. **Flowers:** June – Sept.
Habital: calcareous Alps, rocky debris, 1500 – 2800 m.
Special remarks: Poisonous!

Date Seen: **Place:**

Glacier Crowfoot

Ranunculus glacialis   Buttercup Family; † ⚠

Characters: perennial rosete, bisexual, fie white nectaries often tinged with purple, umbrella-like cluster, 5 green sepals; stem prostrate to upright, thick, leaves alternate, composite, height 5 – 15 cm. **Flowers:** July – Aug. **Habitat:** rocky debris, rock, 2300 – 4200 m. **Distribution:** Alps, Pyrenees, Iceland. **Special Ramarks:** Poisonous! Protected! Medicinal herb.

Date Seen: **Place:**

Christmas Rose

Helleborus niger   Buttercup Family; † ⚠

Characters: perennial, solitary white flowers, 1 – 3 scaly bracts on stem; overwintering leaves, 7 – 6-parted, balck rootstock, height 15 – 30 cm. **Flowers**: Dec.-Apr. **Habitat**: woods, 0 – 1800 m. **Distribution**: calcareous Alps, Apennines, Balkans. **Special Remarks**: Poisonous! Protected! Seeks out limestone.

Date Seen: **Place:**

Narcissus-Flowered Anemone

Anemone narcissiflora Buttercup Family; † ⚠

Characters: perennial, white often pink-flushed below, umbels of 3 – 8 flowers in a many.lobed, bract, 5 – 6 petals; leaves palmately parted, stem and leaf underside hairy, height 30 – 60 cm. **Flowers:** May – July. **Habitat:** woods, brush, 1500 – 2500 m. **Distribution:** calcareous Alps. **Special Remarks:** Protected! Poisonous!

Date Seen: **Place:**

Alpine Moon Daisy

Leucanthemopsis alpina   Daisy Family

Characters: perennial cushion plant, bisexual, flower-heads with white rays, yellow tubular florets, leaves opposite, 1-pinnate, rhizome, height 5 – 15 cm. **Flowers:** July – Aug. **Habitat:** short grass, rocky places, 1600 – 3900 m. **Distribution:** Alps, Pyrenees, Carpathians.

Date Seen: **Place:**

Mountian Avens

Dryas octopetala   Rose Family

Characters: perennial dwarf-shrub, bisexual, solitary flowers with 8 petals, achene with shaggy white papus (flight organ), flowers white; leaves elliptical, evergreen, scalloped, white – woolly beneath, taproot, height 3 – 10 cm.
Flowers: May – Aug. **Habitat:** screes, rock, 1100 – 2500 m. **Distribution:** Northern Europe, Alps, on limestone, dolomite, common.

Date Seen :   **Place:**

Blue Saxifrage

Saxifraga caesia   Saxifrage Family

Characters: perennial cushion plant, white, 5 petals, 1 – 6 flowers per stalk with sticky glandular secretion; leaves in rosettes, small, 5 – 9 limestone pores or entrirely lime encrusted, thick leaves, height 5 – 10 cm. **Flowers:** July – Sept. **Habitat:** rock crevices, screes, 500 – 2500 m, pioneer plant. **Distribution:** calcareous Alps.

Date Seen: **Place:**

Mossy Saxifrage

Saxifraga bryoides   Saxifrage Family; ⚠

Characters: perennial flat cushion plant, white, center yellow, 5 petals, stalk with 1 – 3 flowers; glandular hairs on stalk, leaves rigid, oblong lance-shaped, unnotched, height 1 – 5 cm. **Flowers:** June – Aug. **Habitat:** rocky and stony places, to 2400 m. **Distribution:** only Central Alps. **Special Remarks:** Protected!

Date Seen: **Place:**

Alpine Mouse Ear
Cerastium alpinum   Pink Family

Characters: perennial creeper, white, 5 petals cleft, 1 – 3 flowers at base of leaves; leaves oval, entire plant hairy, height 5 – 20 cm. **Flowers:** July-Sept. **Habitat:** rocky places, 1800 – 2800 m. **Distribution:** Alps, Northern Europe.

Date Seen: **Place:**

Swiss Rock Jasmine

Androsace helvetica   Primrose Family; ⚠

Characters: perennial cushion plant, cushion very dense, 5 white petals with yellow eye, stemless flowers; leaves oval, entire plant hairy, grayish height 1 – 12 cm. **Flowers:** May – July. **Habitat:** rocks, 1500 – 3500 m. **Distribution:** western calcareous Alps. **Special Remarks:** Protected!

Date Seen: **Place:**

Alpine Butterwort

Pinguicula alpina   Butterwort Family; ⚠

Characters: perennial, erect rosette, bisexual, solitary flower spurred, yellow spots in throat, white; leaves oblong, margins inrolled, basal rosette, rhizome, height 5 – 15 cm.
Flowers: May – June. **Habitat:** bogs, wet grasslands, on limestone, 800 – 2000 m. **Distribution:** Alps, Alpine foothills, rare. **Special Remarks:** insectivorous, protected!

Date Seen: **Place:**

Edelweiss

Leontopodium alpinum Daisy Family; ⚠

Characters: perennial rosette, bisexual, flowers packed in compound heads surrounded by woolly-white bracts, only disc of tubular florets, white; leaves lance-shaped, woolly, alternate, height 5 – 20 cm. **Flowers:** July – Aug. **Habitat:** grasslands, dry grasslands, pastures, rock,, 1700 – 3500 m. **Distribution:** Alps, Pyrenees. **Special Remarks:** Entirely protected! Medicinal herb.

Date Seen: **Place:**

Stemless Carline Thistle

Carlina acaulis Daisy Family; ⚠

Characters: perennial rosette, bisexual, disc of brownish tubular florets, outer bracts resemble rays, silvery white; leaves in rosette, pinnately cut, spiny, taproot, height 5 – 30 cm. **Flowers:** July – Sept. **Habitat:** meadows, forests, grasslands, 700 – 2900 m. **Distribution :** Europe, common. **Special Remarks:** Protected!

Date Seen: **Place:**

Scheuchzer's Cotton Sedge

Eriophorum scheuchzeri   Sedge Family

Characters: monocotyledonous, loose, with runners, bi-sexual, spikes with hairy white tuft; stalk cylindrical, upper-most leaf sheathes stalk, short and wide leaf surface, height 15 – 30 cm. **Flowers:** July-Aug. **Habitat:** ponds, waterways, 1500 – 2600 m. **Distribution:** Alps.

Date Seen: **Place:**

✓
Globeflower

Trollius europaeus   Buttercup Family; † ⚠

Characters: perennial, erect, bisexual palnt, 10 petals, 5 – 10 sepals, spherical when closed, yellow; leaves palmately cut, alternate, rizhome, height 10 – 55 cm. **Flowers:** May – Aug. **Habitat:** damp meadows, bogs, tall herb communities, 900 – 2500 m. **Distribution:** Europe. **Special Remarks:** Poisonous! Partially protected! Seeks out nitrogen.

Date Seen: **Place:**

Wolfsbane

Aconitum vulparia Buttercup Family; † ⚠

Characters: perennial, erect plant, bisexual, yellow, helmet-like flowers in raceme, leaves alternate, palmately cut, lower leaves long-stemmed, tarproot, height 50 – 110 cm. **Flowers:** June – Aug. **Habitat:** damp forests, grasslands, 1500 – 2500 m. **Distribution:** Alps, Apennines, not common. **Special Remarks:** Highly piosonous! Protected!

Date Seen: **PlaceRhate:**

Rhaetian Poppy

Papaver alpinum ssp. rhaeticum Poppy Family; ⚠

Characters: perennial with solitary yellow flower, 4 petals roundish, many stamens; stalk erect, bristly, unbranched, basal leaves pinnate, plant with milky latex, height 5 – 15 cm.
Flowers: July- Aug. **Habitat:** screes, 1800 – 3000 m.
Distribution: only Western Alps. **Special Remarks:** in south-east locations narrow-lobed, reddish, in Northern Alps white! Protected!

Date Seen: **Place:**

Alpine Avens

Geum montanum

Rose Family

Characters perennial, creeping rosette, yellow, 5 petals, mainly solitary flowers, hairy, leaves short-stemmed, pinnate, end leaflet largest, friut with long, hairy styles, height 5 – 40 cm. **Flowers:** May – July. **Habitat:** under-fertilized meadows, pastures, dwarf-shrub heath, frost- and windsensitive, 1000 – 3000 m. **Distribution:** Alps, Central Alps.

Date Seen: **Place:**

Aricula

Primula auricula Primrose Family; ⚠

Characters: perennial rosette, bisexual, flower of joined petals, yellow, 4 – 12 flowers per stalk; leaves broad, fleshy, grayish-green, mealy, rihzome, height 5 – 20 cm. **Flowers:** Apr. – June. **Habitat:** stony siol, gravel, rock, 800 – 2600 m. **Distribution:** Alps, Apennines, Carpathians, rare. **Special Remarks:** Endangered! Protected!

Date Seen: **Place:**

Spotted Gentian

Gentiana punctata　　　　　　　　Gentian Family; ⚠

Characters: perennial, erect plant, bisexual, flowers bell-shaped, pale yellow with purple spots, whorled, sepal tube with 5 variously long lobes; leaves oval to oblong, tip never round, rizhome, height 20 – 60 cm. **Flowers:** July – Aug. **Habitat:** stony loam, Alpine dwarf-shrub heath, avoids nitrogen, 1500 – 2500 m. **Distribution:** Alps, particulary acid rocks. **Special Remarks:** Protected! Old medicinal herb.

Date Seen:　　　　　　**Place:**

Artemisia genipi

Artemisia genipi   Daisy Family

Characters: perennial plant, 5 – 30 flowerheads in a leafy spike with leaves, flowerheads nodding at blossom, 10 – 20 yellowish-white solitary blossoms, 1 – 3 cm long, palmate leaves with 3 – 5 clefts, stem leaves pinnate, height 5 – 15 cm. **Flowers:** July – Sept. **Habitat:** rocky, moist-cool soil, moraines, rock fissures, 2000 – 3500 m. **Distribution:** Maritime Alps to Hohe Tauern. **Special Remarks:** Contians less volatile oils than the Yellow Genipi (Artemisia mutellina).

Date Seen: **Place:**

Arnica ✓

Arnica montana   Daisy Family; † ⚠

Characters: perennial, erect plant, bisexual, flowerhead of yellow disc florets with yellow rays, ovary with crown of hairs; stem downy, 1 – 2 pairs of opposite stem leaves, basal leaves oval, in rosettes, tough, hairy aromatic, rhizome, height 20 – 60 cm. **Flowers:** June – Aug. **Habitat:** meadows, woods, grasslands, peaty soil, 200 – 2900 m. **Distribution:** Alps, Apennines, Carpathians. **Special Remarks:** Endangered! Protected! Pisosonous! Medicinal herb – demands great caution!

Date Seen: **Place:**

Large Flowered Leopardsbane

Doronicum grandiflorum   Daisy Family

Characters: perennial, erect plant, bisexual, disc of yellow tubular florets with yellow rays; leaves alternate, clasping stalk, glandular-hairy, rizhome, height 10 – 50 cm. **Flowers:** July – Aug. **Habitat:**screes, rock crevices, 1700 – 3200 m. **Distribution:** calcareous Alps, Pyrenees, Corsica, not common.

Date Seen: **PLace:**

Golden Hawksbeard

Crepis aurea   Daisy Family

Characters: perennial, rosette, orange-yellow rays form solitary flowers, flower bracts and upper stem with dark green hairs; leaves hairless, lance-shaped, toothed, height 20 – 30 cm. **Flowers:** July – Sept. **Habitat:** meadows, pastures, 1000 – 2500 m. **Distribution:** Alps,northern Balkan peninsula

Date Seen: **PLace:**

Chamois Ragwort

Senecio doronicum   Daisy Family

Characters: perennial, flowerheads of yellow rays and disc of tubular florets, 1 – 8 in loose raceme, downy, leaves long and narrow, downy, lightly toothed, height 20 – 50 cm. **Flowers:** July – Aug. **Habitat:** grassy and rocky places, screes, on limestone, 1000 – 3000 m. **Distribution:** calcareous Alps.

Date Seen: **Place:**

Gray Alpine Groundsel

Senecio incanus ssp. carniolicus   Daisy Famliy

Characters: perennial, yellow flowerheads with 3 – 6 rays, yellow tubular florets, heads in umbels; leaves slightly feathered (pinnate) or scalloped, gray-green, height 15 cm.
Flowers: July – Sept. **Habitat:** grasslands, screes, rock, over 2000 m. **Distribution:** east of the Grisons (Graubünden), Allgäu.

Date Seen: **Place:**

Giant Catser

Hypochoeris uniflora   Daisy Family

Characters: perennial rosette, only yellow rays forming one flowerhead per stem, stem swollen under flowerhead, roughly hairy, sepal with dark hairs; leaves sparsely hairy, toothed, height 30 – 50 cm. **Flowers:** July – Sept. **Habitat:** acid soils, mountain forests, seeks out acid soils, 1000 – 2500 m. **Distribution:** Central and Southern Alps.

Date Seen: **Place:**

Retuse-Leaved Willow

Salix retusa   Willow Family

Characters: dioecious, mat-forming undershrub with rooting branches, few flowers in loose catkins, yellow; leaves twice as long as wide, tip blunt or notched, hairless, dark green, later yellow. **Flowers:** June – Oct. **Habitat:** acid soils, mountain forests, seeks out acid soils, 1500 – 2500 m. **Distribution:** Alps, Pyrenees, Apennines.

Date Seen: **Place:**

Mountain Houseleek ✓

Sempervivum montanum Stonecrop Family; ⚠

Characters: perennial rosette with runners, bisexual, dark red to pink, 12-16 petals, flowerheads in umbel; stem and fleshly stem leaves glandular hairy, basal leaves forming small dense rosettes, height 5 – 15 cm. **Flowers:** July – Aug **Habitat:** stony places, rocks, 1900 – 3500 m. **Distribution:** Alps, Apennines, Pyrenees. **Special Remarks:** Protected!

Date Seen: **Place:**

Purple Saxifrage

Saxifraga oppositifolia   Saxifrage Family; ⚠

Characters: perennial cushion plant, flowers bloom red, fade to blue, 5 petals, trailing stem covered with 4 conspicuous rows of dense leaves; leaves opposite, rigid, height 2 – 5 cm. **Flowers:** Mar. – July. **Habitat:** stony grasslands, rock, mountian crests, 1700 – 3500 m. **Distribution:** Alps, Scandinavia. **Special Remarks:** Protected!

Date Seen: **Place:**

Alpine Rock Jasmine
Androsace alpina　　　　　　　　　Primrose Family; ⚠

Characters: perennial, bisexual cushion plant with taproot, pink to red, also white, solitary flowers with 5 petals; basal, lance-shaped leaves, height 2 – 6 cm. **Flowers:** July – Aug. **Habitat:** screes, 2000 – 4200 m. **Distribuion:** Alps. **Special Remarks:** Protected!

Date Seen:　　　　　　**Place:**

Moss Campion

Silene acaulis   Pink Family; ⚠

Characters: perennial, cushion plant, bisexual, red solitary flowers with 5 petals, sepals fused; leaves lance-shaped, short, margin ciliated, taproot, height to 5 cm. **Flowers:** June – Aug. **Habitat:** grasslands, rock, screes, 1900 – 3200 m. **Distribution:** Alps, Apennines, Pyrenees, common. **Special Remarks:** Protected!

Date Seen: **Place:**

39

Alpenrose

Rhododendron ferrugineum Heather Family; ⚠

Characters: shrub, bisexual, flowers funnel-shaped, solitary flowers in umbel at end of stem, dark red, sometimes paler or white; leaves evergreen, oval, margins rolled under, reddish gland scales beneath, height 50 – 150 cm. **Flowers:** May – Aug. **Habitat:** pine forests, 1500 – 2400 m. **Distribution:** Central Alps, Pyrenees, Apennines. **Special Remarks:** Partially protectedt!

Date Seen: **Place:**

Hairy Alpenrose

Rhododendron hirsutum Heahter Family; ⚠

Characters: shrub, pale red, hairy, funnel-shaped flowers, inside white, terminal clusters, 5-lobed flowers; leaves leathery, shiny yellow, later brown scaly galnds, margin conspiciously hairy, height 50 – 20 cm. **Flowers:** May – Aug. **Habitat:** screes, dwarf-shrub heath, anchors debris, 1200 – 2400 m. **Distribution:** calcareous Alps. **Special Remarks:** Protected!

Date Seen: **Place:**

41

Creeping Azalea ✓

Loiseleuria procumbens   Heather Family

Characters: prostrate, mat-forming undershrub, 2 – 5 flowers at the end of shoot, red, 5-lobed flower, conspicuously
bellshaped, anthers dark red; leaves leathery, opposite,
margins rolled under, height 15 – 30 cm. **Flowers:** June –
July. **Habitat:** stony places, 1500 – 2500 m. **Distribution:**
European mountains, Arctic, pioneer plant.

Date Seen: **Place:**

Spring Heath

Erica carnea   Heather Family; ⚠

Characters: dwarf undershrub, bisexual, flowers small, bell-shaped, 4-lobed, with projecting anthers, flesh-pink; leaves linear in whorls around stem, height 15 – 40 cm. **Flowers:** Jan. – Apr. **Habitat:** dwarf-shrub heath, screes, 1500 – 2200m. **Distribution:** Alps, Apennines, on limestone. **Special Remarks:** Partially protected!

Date Seen: **Place:**

Least Primrose ✓

Primula minima   Primrose Family; ⚠

Characters: perennial rosette, bisexual, solitary flowers, 5 red petals fused to tubes, tips of petals spread like open saucers, petals deeply notched, white eye, 5 fused sepals; leaves pale green, apex toothed, glossy, not sticky, rhizome, height to 3 cm. **Flowers:** June – July. **Habitat:** dry grasslands, rock, 1200 – 3100 m. **Distribution:** Alps, Carpathians, Balkans, rare. **Special Remarks:** Endangered! Protected!

Date Seen: **Place:**

Sowbread

Cyclamen purpurascens   Primerose Family; ⚠

Characters: perennial, carmine pink, fragrant, solitary flowers, 5 reflexed petals, drooping, flower coiled in friut; leaves evergreen, heart- or kidney-shaped, slightly scalloped, dark green with lighter, shiny pattern, height 5 – 20 cm.
Flowers: June – Sep. **Habitat:** woods, brushland, 1000 – 1500 m. **Distribution:** calcareous Alps. **Special Remarks:** Protected!

Date Seen: **Place:**

Mountian Thrift

Armeria alpina   Thrift Family; ⚠

Characters: perennial rosette bush, bisexual, flowers in capitulum, bracts scarious, pink to red; basal leaves, narrow, grassy, three longitudinal veins, taproot, height 5 – 20 cm.
Flowers: May – Oct. **Habitat:** screes, dry grasslands, rock, 1100 – 3100 m. **Distribution:** Alps, Pyrenees, Eastern Carpathians. **Special Remarks:** Protected!

Date Seen: **Place:**

Garland Flower

Daphne striata   Daphne Family; † ⚠

Characters: perennial bush, bisexual, 4 petals fused to tube, 8 – 12 flowers in terminal clusters, pink; leaves evergreen, wedge-shaped, crowded at shoot tips, height 5 – 35 cm. **Flowers:** May – July. **Habitat:** screes, stony grasslands, rock, 1500 – 2500 m. **Distribution:** absent from Central Alps, rare. **Specail Remarks:** Poisonous! Protected!

Date Seen: **Place:**

Crimson-Tipped Lousewort

Pedicularis oederi   Figwort Family; †

Characters: perennial semiparasite, 5 – 15 pale yellow flowers in dense raceme, purple spots on upper lip, untoothed, lower lip spreading, hairless; leaves pinnate and finely toothed, height 5 – 20 cm. **Flowers:** June – July. **Habitat:** grasslands, dwarf-shrub heath, 1500 – 2500 m. **Distribution:** calcareous Alps. **Special Remarks:** Poisonous!

Date Seen: **Place:**

Flesh-Pink Lousewort

Pedicularis rostrato-spicata   Figwort Family; †

Characters: perennial, 3 – 15 flowers forming dense cluster, dark pink, flower angled at 90°, lower lip slightly spreading, upper lip with small beak; stem leaves alternate, leaves pinnate and serrated, height 20 – 40 cm. **Flowers:** July – Aug. **Habitat:** grasslands, 1800 – 2300 m. **Distribution:** calcareous Alps. **Special Remarks:** Poisonous!

Date Seen: **Place:**

Wolly Thistle
Cirsium eriophorum   Daisy Family

Characters: perennial, erect, bisexual, red-purple to pale purple tubular flowers clustered to 7-cm-tall flowersheads; bracts enveloped in white cobwebby wool with prickles, stem white cottony, leaves white cottony beneath, long spines, pinnate, margin partly inrolled, green above, height 60 – 100 cm. **Flowers:** July – Sep. **Habitat:** pastures, waysides, grasslands, 600 – 2300 m. **Distribution:** Europe.

Date Seen: **Place:**

Martagon Lily
Lilium martagon   Lily Family; ⚠

Characters: monocotyledonous perennial, erect, bisexual, flower purple, pink, white, 6-parted, drooping petals, loose raceme, petals recurved; leaves whorled, unnotched, oval, bulb, height 30 – 100 cm. **Flowers:** June – Aug. **Habitat:** meadows, woods, grasslands, 200 – 2500 m. **Distribution:** Alps, Apennines, Caucasus Mountains, common. **Special Remarks:** Protected! Medicinal herb.

Date Seen: **Place:**

Orange Lily
Lilium bulbiferum   Lily Family; ⚠

Characters: perennial, monocotyledonous bulb plant, bright orange, 6 petals with black spots inside, solitary or clustered flowers; leaves narrow, spiraling, upright, height 30 – 90 cm. **Flowers:** June – July. **Habitat:** pastures, grasslands, screes, woods, 300 – 2000 m. **Distribution:** Central and South Europe. **Special Remarks:** Endangered! Protected!

Date Seen: **Place:**

Black Vanilla Orchid

Nigritella nigra   Orchid Family; ⚠

Characters: monocotyledonous perennial, bisexual, flowers blackish-purple, spires; leaves lance-shaped, alternate, tuber, height 10 – 20 cm. **Flowers:** June – Aug. **Habitat:** pastures, grasslands, 1200 – 2700 m. **Distribution:** Europe, rare. **Special Remarks:** Endangered! Protected! Medicinal herb.

Rosy Vanilla Orchid

Nigritella rosea   ⚠

Pink flower. **Special Remarks:** Protected! Endangered!

Date Seen: **Place:**

Jaquin's Rush
Juncus jaquinii   Rush Family

Characters: inconspicuous solitary flowers, blackish-brown, anthers yellow, stigmas red and spiraling, flowers in capitulum, stalked; stem and leaves cylindrical, plant forms dense turf, height 15 – 25 cm. **Flowers:** July – Oct. **Habitat:** moors, damp places, 1700 – 3000 m. **Distribution:** Central Alps.

Date Seen: **Place:**

Netted Willow

Salix reticulata　　　　　　　　　　Willow Family; ⚠

Characters: creeping, strongly branched undershrub, dioecious, long-stalked, catkins rusty-red; leaves green, net-veined, hairy, height 3 – 8 cm. **Flowers:** July – Aug. **Habitat:** cushion sedge grasslands, dwarf-shrub heath, 1700 – 2500 m. **Distribution:** Alps, Pyrenees, Jura Mountains. **Special Remarks:** Partially protected!

Date Seen:　　　　　　**Place:**

Common Monkshood

Aconitum napellus   Buttercup Family; †

Characters: perennial, erect bush, flower of violet sepals, helmet-shaped, without spurs, petals form nectary; leaves large, pamately cut, 5 – 7 parted, dark green above, pale green beneath, shiny, tunrip-shaped root, height 50 – 180 cm. **Flowers:** June – Aug. **Habitat:** tell-herb communities, damp places, to 2000 m. **Distribution:** Southern and Central European mountians. **Special Remarks:** Seeks out nitrogen. Highly poisonous! Do not pick! Medicinal herb.

Date Seen: **Place:**

Small Pasque Flower

Pulsatilla alpina   Buttercup Family; † ⚠

Characters: perennial rosette, bisexual, 5-to many-parted solitary flowers, dark violet; basal leaves, pinnate, rhizome, height 10 – 25 cm. **Flowers:** Mar.-May. **Habitat:** dry grasslands, 200 – 1500 m. **Distribution:** Alps, Carpathians, Balkans, rare. **Special Remarks:** Poisonous! Protected! Medicinal herb, demands care in use!

Date Seen: **Place:**

Spring Pasque Flower

Pulsatilla vernalis   Buttercup Family; † ⚠

Characters: perennial, flower violet outside, thite inside, hairy, funnel-shaped bract with amny lobes; leaves and stem hairy, leaves leathery, 1-pinnate or 3-parted, height 5 – 20 cm. **Flowers:** Apr. – July. **Habitat:** grasslands, dry grasslands, stony soils, to 3500 m. **Distribution:** Alps, Scandinavia, avoids limestone. **Special Remarks:** Poisonous! Protected!

Date Seen: **Place:**

Sticky Primrose

Primula glutinosa   Primerose Family; ⚠

Characters: perennial, purple to violet, 2 – 7 flowers per-stem, 5 petals fused to tube, lobes open saucers; leaves with dark spots above, toothed, entire plant sticky, height 2 – 8 cm. **Flowers:** July – Aug. **Habitat:** screes, curved sedge grasslands, 1600 – 3000 m. **Distribution:** Eastern Alps. **Special Remarks:** Protected!

Date Seen: **Place:**

Alpine Snowbell

Soldanella alpina   Primerose Family

Characters: perennial rosette, bisexual, 1 – 3 flowers, deeply fringed, 5 throat scales, styles longer than flower, violet;
leaves rounded to kidney-shaped, basal, height 5 – 15 cm.
Flowers: Apr. – June. **Habitat:** snowbeds, damp pastures,
900 – 1800 m. **Distribution:** Alps, Apennines, Pyrenees.

Date Seen: 18 . 6 . 09   **Place:**

German Gentian

Gentiana germanica Gentian Family; ⚠

Characters: perennial rosette, reddish-violet, 5 oval lanci-form petals, bearded throat, many flowers at base of leaves and at end of shoots; leaves opposite, oval, rosette leaves generally dead at blossom, height 5 – 40 cm. **Flowers:** Aug. – Oct. **Habitat:** limestone-rich, sometimes moist grass-lands, 300 – 2000 m. **Distribution:** northern and southern cal-careous Alps. **Special Remarks:** Protected! Endangered!

Date Seen: **Place:**

Alpine Toadflax

Linaria alpina   Figwort Family

Characters: perennial, bluish- to reddish-violet always with orange patch, 2 – 8 flowers in small raceme, long spur; leaves unnotched, whorled, lance-shaped, rooting stem, height 5 – 10 cm. **Flowers:** June – July. **Habitat:** screes, anchors debris, 1500 – 3000 m. **Distribution:** calcareous Alps.

Date Seen: 20. 6. 09   **Place:**

Round-Headed Rampion

Phyteuma orbiculare   Bellflower Family

Characters: biennial, flowers pale blue-violet, with strap-sha-
ped lobes joined at base, many solitary flowers in terminal
head, style protrudes from flowers; stalked, oval-oblong ab-
sal leaves, height 10 – 40 cm. **Flowers:** May – Sept. **Habitat:**
grasslands, open woods, 0 – 2000 m. **Distribution:** calcareous Alps.

Date Seen: 20·6·09   **Place:**

Alpine Aster
Aster alpinus   Daisy Family

Characters: perennial rosette, bisexual, composite head, violet rays, disc of yellow tubular florets; leaves alternate, narrow, rhizome, height 5 – 20 cm. **Flowers:** July – Aug. **Habitat:** pastures, grasslands, screes, rock, 1400 – 3000 m. **Distribution:** Alps, Apennines, Carpathians, common.

Date Seen: 20 6 09   **Place**

Tassel Hyacinth

Muscari comosum   Lily Family; ⚠

Characters: perennial, monocotyledonous, bulb, blue-violet, long-stemmed bells in raceme; basal leaves in rosette, lance-shaped, height 20 – 70 cm. **Flowers:** Apr. – June. **Habitat:** meadows, dry grasslands, rocky soil, to 1500 m. **Distribution:** Southern, Western Europe. **Special Remarks:** Protected! Endangered! Medicinal herb.

Date Seen: **Place:**

Alpine Clematis

Clematis alpina   Buttercup Family; ⚠

Characters: perennial climber, bisexual, flowers, solitary, nodding at base of leaf, petals form white nectary, 4 – 5 sepals (blue) form flower; leavesalternate, 1-2-pinnate, hairy beneath, tendril-like leaf stems, height 2 – 4 m. **Flowers:** May – July. **Habitat:** mountain forests, brushwood, rare, on limestone, 1000 – 1400 m. **Distribution:** Alps, Pyrenees, Apennines. **Special Remarks:** Protected!

Date Seen: **Place:**

Alpine Eryngo
Eryngium alpinum   Carrot Family; ⚠

Characters: perennia, bisexual, umbel-like cluster of 2 – 4 cylindrical heads, flowers small, blue, spiny bracts; 3-parted stem leaves, basal leaves undivided, all leaves spiny, turnip-like root, height 30 – 60 cm. **Flowers:** July – Sept. **Habitat:** grasslands, pastures, 1500 – 2500 m. **Distribution:** Southern and Western Alps. **Special Remarks:** Rare, strictly protected! Endangered!

Date Seen: **Place:**

Clusius's Gentian

Gentiana clusii   Gentian Family; ⚠

Characters: perennial rosette, bisexual, flowers solitary trumpets, 5 – 6 cm, azure blue, inside no green spots, almost no stem, sepal teeth triangular, no white membrane; leaves oval to oblong, rhizome, height 8 cm. **Flowers:** May – Aug. **Habitat:** rare, often in soil rich in lime, in cushion sedge grasslands, blue-grass, 1200 – 2800 m. **Distribution:** Alps, Apennines, Carpathians. **Special Remarks:** Protected!

Date Seen   **Place:**

Trumpet Gentian

Gentiana acaulis   Gentian Family; ⚠

Characters: perennial, bisexual, rosette, dark blue, large erect flowers, inside always with green stripe; basal leaves in rosette, broad, height 5 – 10 cm. **Flowers:** May-Aug. **Habitat:** grasslands, meadows, 800 – 3100 m. **Distribution:** Alps, Apennines. **Special Remarks:** Endangered! Protected! Old medicinal herb.

Date Seen: 19·6·09   **Place:**

Spring Gentian
Gentiana verna Gentian Family; ⚠

Characters: perennial rosette, bisexual, bright blue solitary flowers, tight petal tube with lobes in open saucer, sepal lobed tube; on upright stem 1 – 3 pairs of smaller, opposite leaves, basal leaves elliptical to lance-shaped, rhizome, height 5 – 10 cm. **Flowers:** Apr. – Aug. **Habitat:** mountian meadows, semi-dry grasslands, 300 – 2700 m. **Distribution:** Alps, Apennines, Pyrenees, common. **Special Remarks:** Completely protected!

Date Seen: 18.6.09   **Place:**

Willow-Leaved Gentian

Gentiana asclepiadea   Gentian Family; ⚠

Characters: perennial, erect plant, bisexual, bell-shaped flowers, with short stems from base of upper leaves, 5-lobed, bright blue, inside pale stripes or spots; leaves oval, lance-shaped, decussate (in alternate pairs), rhizome, height 30 – 70 cm. **Flowers:** July – Sept. **Habitat:** damp mountain meadows and grasslands. **Distribution:** calcareous Alps. **Special Remarks:** Completely protected!

Date Seen: **Place:**

Wulfenia

Wulfenia carinthiaca　　　　　　　　　　　Figwort Family

Characters: perennial rosette, bluish-violet, solitary flower approx. 1.5 cm, blossoms in spikes dipping to one side, stem with scaly leaves, leaves to 15 cm with notched lobes. **Flowers:** July – Aug. **HAbitat:** moist humusrich grasslands over acid rocks, 1000 – 2000 m. **Distribution:** endemic, Gail Valley Alps.

Date Seen:　　　　　　　　　**Place:**

Bearded Bellflower

Campanula barbata   Bellflower Family

Characters: perennial rosette, bisexual, blue or white, bell-shaped, 5-lobed hairy flowers in loose raceme; leaves basal, narrow, height 10 – 30 cm. **Flowers;** June – Aug. **Habitat:** meadows, grasslands, woods, 1000 – 3000 m. **Distribution:** Alps, Southern, Central Europe.

Date Seen: **Place:**

Scheuchzer's Bellflower

Campanula scheuchzeri   Bellflower Family

Characters: perennial, dark blue, bells somewhat crowded, 5-lobed, terminal or in terminal racemes; stem hairless, stem leaves lance-shaped, hairy-edged at base, basal leaves rounded to heart-shaped, height 3 – 15 cm. **Flowers:** June – Sept. **Habitat:** stony places, grasslands, dwarf-shrub heath, screes, to over 3000 m. **Distribution:** Alps, Pyrenees.

Date Seen: Place:

Fairy's Thimble

Campanula cochlearifolia   Bellflower Family

Characters: perennial, rosette, creeper, bisexual, nodding, racemes of blue-violet flowers, outside dark-veined; leaves alternate, lance-shaped, rhizome, height 5 – 15 cm. **Flowers:** June – Aug. **Habitat:** screes, rock, 1300 – 3500 m. **Distribution:** Alps, Apennines, Balkans, common.

Date Seen: **Place:**

Matted Globularia
Globularia cordifolia   Bellflower Family

Characters: perennial, creeping dwarf subshrub, bisexual, 7 mm long, head of bell-shaped flowers, upper lip 2-lobed, lower lip 3-lobed, pale blue to white; basal leaves, oblong, never round at tip, rhizome, height 3 – 15 cm. **Flowers:** May – Aug. **Habitat:** dry grasslands, screes, rock, 1800 – 2500 m, on limestone, likes warmth. **Distribution:** Alps, Apennines, Balkans.

Date Seen: 20·6·09   **Place:**

Spiniest Thistle

Cirsium spinosissimum   Daisy Family

Characters: perennial, bisexual, flowerhead only disc florets, no rays, pale green, long pointed bracts; leaves alternate along entire stalk, spine-toothed, feathery, cylindrical root, height to 120 cm. **Flowers:** July – Sept. **Habitat:** damp pastures, screes, cirques, 1600 – 3000 m. **Distribution:** Alps. **Special Remarks:** Seeks out nitrogen.

Date Seen: **Place:**

Index
of English Names:

Index
of Scientific Names:

KOMPASS

Austrian Specialties

www.kompass.at